The heart-traveller

4

Sri Chinmoy

New Year's Messages
From Sri Chinmoy
(1966-2007)

Ganapati Press

© 2022 SRI CHINMOY CENTRE

ISBN 978-1-911319-44-3

Cover drawing: Soul-Bird by C.K.G.

FIRST EDITION WENT TO PRESS ON 7 December 2022

New Year's Messages
From Sri Chinmoy
(1966-2007)

1966

May humanity climb one rung up in the ladder of divine growth, and realise in its soul the Sweetness, Joy, Light and Peace of the Supreme.

Out of the pure fulness of the heart, may the lips of truth speak and the hands of truth act in the year 1966.

The New Year – what can it teach us? It can teach us the secret of spiritual self-reliance. It can teach us how we ourselves can be our masters and saviours.

From the New Year we can learn that God is God only when God is *our* God and not *my* God. From the New Year we can learn that truth is truth only when truth is *our* truth and not *my* truth.

At every moment it is we who can make ourselves a blessing to ourselves and to the world at large.

May the universal embrace of the New Year flower into a permanent Smile of Victory on the

Face of the Supreme.

1967

Arise! Your Lord Supreme is crying for you.

Awake! Your Lord Supreme is waiting for you in the Sea of Transcendental Consciousness.

Walk! Your Lord Supreme is expecting your sure and safe arrival.

March! It is you who will realise your Lord Supreme in this very life.

Run! It is you who will fulfil your Lord Supreme in this life of yours here on earth.

Fly! Yours is the Goal of the ever-transcending Beyond.

1968

A new year dawns. A new year, a new aspiration, a new dedication and a new realisation enter into us. Let us enter into the Supreme with a new joy, a new achievement and a new, constantly surrendering attitude. We are always fond of the new. Tomorrow, on New Year's Day, that new newness will enter into us. What can we expect from tomorrow? We expect that which we do not have right now: freedom from bondage, freedom from limitation, freedom from disease, freedom from death. Our expectation is not enough. In addition to our expectation, we must cultivate deep within us the firm determination that we shall have it, that we are bound to have all these divine qualities.

I always say, "The past is dust." Once again I repeat, "The past is dust." Why? The past has not given us what we have been striving for. So the past is of no use. It is the present, and the golden future which enters into the present, which make us feel what we are going to be – nay, what we truly are. We are not children of the past, but children of the glorious future.

There are many things that we want to do, that we want to achieve. But unfortunately we have not been able to achieve them. Why? Because our aspiration is not intense, our determination is not firm, our cry, our inner cry, is not genuine. Yet there is no end to the progress we can make, and each new year comes and stands in front of us to remind us of that very fact: that there is no end to our progress, both inner progress and outer progress.

How can we transcend ourselves? We can transcend ourselves the moment we feel that self-realisation or the conquest of the self is our birthright, our divine heritage. It is not that somebody has to come and thrust upon us this divine heritage.

We have to leave aside, cast aside, throw aside doubt, one of our greatest enemies. Doubt does not allow us to go one inch forward or one inch backward. When we want to look forward, doubt says, "No, you are not so good." And when we want to look back, a kind of subtle doubt again tells us, "No, you cannot be so bad." Doubt never, never allows us to see the truth, to know where we actually stand. We stand right in front of God. And where are we seated? We are seated in the Lap of the Supreme.

Let us cry. The world needs seekers who will cry like a child for the Mother. We have forgotten how to cry. We know how to talk, how to impose truth on others, how to convince others of what we have acquired or what we have learned. From today on, let us cry from the inmost recesses of our hearts, Him to possess and Him to reveal. Without the Supreme, we do not exist. It is an unpardonable foolishness on our part when we say that we exist without Him. No, we do not exist, we can never exist even for a second without Him. If you really, sincerely, whole-heartedly care for the truth, then my fervent request to you is to go deep within and try to discover your own divinity.

I am here to be your eternal slave. I shall wash the very dust of your feet the moment you feel that you are prepared to cry, cry wholeheartedly for the Supreme.

All of us present here, all the true members of our spiritual family, must, once and for all, cast aside doubt. We must always feel that we are children of the Supreme. We are growing together, we are fulfilling the Supreme together. The Supreme is entering into us to inspire us to dive into the deepest, to fly into the highest, to run towards the farthest.

In the Name of the Supreme, I bless each and every one present here and all those who are in my boat, who need my help, my guidance, my assistance. It is not just for a year but forever, for Eternity. I shall be a loving, dedicated servant, a slave, to all of you who care for the Supreme and for the Supreme alone. If one says or feels that the Supreme is his or hers, then at that very moment that person can rest assured that I am here to be of immediate service to him.

For me there can be no greater joy, no greater pride, than to serve the seekers of truth. And this is my soul's promise to each of you on the eve of the New Year.

1969

Three hundred and sixty-five opportunities to realise the Supreme, to reveal the Supreme and to fulfil the Supreme.

1970

Whence comes man?
Whither goes he?
He comes forth from God's Aspiration
And enters into God's Perfection.

1971

Nineteen hundred and seventy-one will be the year of divine, supreme manifestation.

Those who have divine obedience will offer their divine obedience to the Supreme.

Those who have divine love will offer their divine love to the Supreme.

Those who have divine devotion will offer their divine devotion to the Supreme.

Those who have divine surrender will offer their divine surrender to the Supreme.

While offering obedience, love, devotion and surrender, the seekers will manifest these divine qualities on earth.

Nineteen hundred and seventy-one is the year of divine manifestation.

Those who have only obedience can feel that they are babies.

Those who have love can feel that they are growing children.

Those who have devotion can feel that they

are now at the adolescent stage.

And those who have surrender can feel that they are strong, stout, determined youth.

Now in surrender, we always say that unconditional surrender and constant surrender are needed. Unconditionally and constantly surrendered seekers are the seekers who can remain on the top of the tree; and those who have surrendered merely for a day or two or for a few minutes are at the foot of the tree.

Others who have devotion, love and obedience are running towards the tree. Among them, obedience comes third. First comes devotion, second, love and third, obedience. But they are all running; they will one day reach the tree. They will stay at the foot of the tree and become surrendered, and then gradually, if it is God's Will, they will become unconditionally and constantly surrendered seekers.

This is the year of manifestation. For those who have faith in God-realisation, this is the year for them to expedite their inner seeking. The year of manifestation is for those who want the Supreme for the Supreme; who want the

Supreme for His sake and not for their sake.

For our disciples, sincere disciples, this year of manifestation will be the year of inner glory in God, glory in the Supreme's highest, transcendental Pride. For the Supreme needs, as we need, many things. He needs totally, unreservedly, unconditionally and constantly surrendered disciples. It is they who will be the torch-bearers of the supreme Truth. The Supreme is inwardly crying for these constantly, unconditionally surrendered disciples.

1972

The New Year is the year of battle between man's inner faith and his outer doubts. Man's sincerity will determine the victory.

The New Year is the year of war between human insecurity and divine confidence. Man's real need of God will determine the victory.

The New Year knows no compromise. Either the divine in us will gain the supreme victory or the animal in us will lord it over us. Needless to say, those who want to be God-lovers, God-discoverers and God-fulfillers will receive from God constant Concern, constant Protection, constant Guidance and constant Assurance.

The New Year is the year of both destruction and perfection. Those who cherish destruction in the depths of their hearts and glorify themselves in it will be embraced and devoured by total destruction. This is the Will of the Transcendental Lord decreed. Those who cry for divine illumination and perfection in their inner and outer lives will be inspired, blessed, illumined, perfected and fulfilled by the Lord Supreme's Supreme Perfection.

The Boat of the Supreme is ready.
The Supreme Boatman is ready.
The Golden Shore is ready.

The Boatman, with His transcendental Smile, beckons,

"Welcome, O God-lover!
Welcome, O God-discoverer!
Welcome, O God-fulfiller!"

1973

The New Year is the year of our mind's inspiration, our heart's creation and our soul's manifestation.

Inspiration will march onward to the Source.

Creation will sit at the pinnacle of enlightenment.

Manifestation will at once prove its divinity and immortality.

The New Year is the year of acceptance and transformation.

The human in us will try to accept the divine in us unconditionally.

The divine in us will transform the human in us untiringly and unconditionally.

In the New Year, every day will be an opportunity for the God-believer to see the truth-light.

In the New Year, every hour will be an opportunity for the God-worshipper to achieve the truth-light.

In the New Year, every second will be an

opportunity for the God-lover to become the truth-light.

1974

In 1974 the seekers of the transcendental Truth shall dive deep within and more within and become the perfection-smile of aspiration-power, realisation-love, revelation-oneness and manifestation-light.

1975

The year 1975 will be the year
Of the seeker's outer success
And inner progress.
With his outer success,
He will love and serve the Supreme Pilot.
With his inner progress,
He will manifest and fulfil the Supreme Pilot.

1976

The New Year will be the year of destruction,
Frustration and satisfaction.
The animal in us will unimaginably be
   destroyed.
The human in us will unreservedly be
   frustrated.
The divine in us will supremely be satisfied.

The animal in us is self-doubt.
The human in us is self-indulgence.
The divine in us is self-offering.

1977

The New Year will be the year
Of our astounding achievements.
Our inner achievement will be peace.
Our outer achievement will be progress.
Peace is realisation-seed.
Progress is satisfaction-fruit.

1978

The heart of the year 1978
Belongs to the aspiration-perfection-sky.
The life of the year 1978
Belongs to the dedication-satisfaction-land.
Heart is humanity's changeless oneness
With God.
Heart is humanity's changing newness
In God.
Life is humanity's crying fulness
In God.
Life is humanity's smiling fulness
For God.

1979

The New Year is the year
Of man and earth's self-giving choice,
And also is the victory-year
Of God's soundless Voice.

1980

For the soulfully sincere seekers
Of the Absolute Supreme,
The year 1980 is the year
Of amazing harmony,
Astounding peace
And abiding oneness.

1981

In 1981
The Supreme Lord will utilise
The soul-beauty,
The heart-purity
And the life-sincerity
Of His seeker-children
For the manifestation
Of His perfect Perfection.

1982

The New Year will be the man-awakening
And the life-illumining God-Hour.
The eyeless will see the Vision-Eye
Of the Absolute Supreme,
And the heartless will feel the
    Compassion-Heart
Of the Absolute Supreme.

1983

The year 1983
Will be the year of the seeker's glory:
Glory within, glory without,
Glory illumining, glory abiding –
A oneness-glory
Between the self-giving seeker
And his life-transforming God.

1984

The seeker's confidence-heart
And the seeker's surrender-life
Shall play together
The complete perfection-game
In God's Vision-Home.

1985

Don't expect!
Don't expect!
Give, give and give
If you want to really survive.

1986

The New Year will be
The year of teeming surprises –
Heaven-descending golden Dreams,
Earth-ascending silver realities –
For the seekers
Who sleeplessly and unconditionally live
For the Compassion-Eye-Manifestation
And
For the Satisfaction-Heart-Manifestation
Of their Beloved Supreme
Throughout the length and breadth
Of the entire world.

1987

For the Mountain-Truth-climbers
And the Fountain-God-lovers
The New Year will be the year
Of unprecedented inner aspiration-progress
And unlimited outer manifestation-success.
The Truth-climber
Is a God-chosen God-compeer.
The God-lover
Is a God-crowned future world-liberator.

1988

My only Lord Beloved Supreme,
Do bless me
With Your absolutely choice,
Secret and sacred Advice
For the New Year.

"My child, win My Heart
And thus win My All —
My Eternity's All,
My Infinity's All
And My Immortality's All."

My only Lord Beloved Supreme,
How can I win Your Heart?

"My child, by loving Me only
And by needing Me only."

My only Lord Beloved Supreme,
How can I love You only?

How can I need You only?

"My child, be punctual in your heart's
Aspiration-cry.
Be regular in your life's
Dedication-smile."

My only Lord Beloved Supreme,
I have badly failed You this year.
I have all along failed You unquestionably.
But, my Lord, will I ever succeed?

"My child, you must and you will.
Just sleeplessly illumine your mind
And convince your heart
That you are of My Eternity's Hunger only
And you are for My Immortality's
Satisfaction only."

My only Lord Beloved Supreme,
I know that my living death will be
When You withdraw from me completely.
But will You ever withdraw from me?

"My child, do not think of My withdrawal,
But pray to Me to be with Me in My Boat
To reach your supreme Destination –
My complete Satisfaction in you, with you
And for you.
I have so far not withdrawn from you.
But,
My child, wake up!
It is already very late.
How long do you expect Me to hold
My Golden Boat
On this side of ignorance-ocean?
You have to realise that either I am your All
Or you are all for yourself
And all by yourself."

1989

From time immemorial
Humanity's heart has been treasuring
Himalayan hope-dreams.

And now, before long,
Divinity's Soul will descend
With satisfaction-realities on earth
And blessingfully quench
The ceaseless peace-thirst,
And compassionately appease
The breathless oneness-hunger
Of the world-family.

Arise! Awake!
Smile soulfully
At tomorrow's fulfilment-flooded
Perfection-Dawn.

1990

My Lord Supreme,
I am now feeling powerfully great
By offering You my mind's gratitude-smiles.
My Beloved Supreme,
I am now feeling breathlessly good
By offering You my heart's gratitude-cries.
My Lord Beloved Supreme,
Out of Your infinite Bounty,
Do share with me a blessingful secret
For the New Year, 1990.

"My child,
My Infinity's Dream-treasuring child,
I shall share with you not one,
But two blessingfully sacred secrets.
Yesterday's self-gratifying
 division-hunger-world
Will before long be buried in oblivion-cave.
My child,
My Immortality's Reality-manifesting child,

Today's self-giving oneness-aspiration-world
Will receive from Me
In the victory-flooded future
My Transcendental Silence-Crown
And My Universal Sound-Throne."

1991

The daring competition-success-might of the human mind is wisely going to surrender to the caring illumination-progress-delight of the divine heart.

The inner voice is whispering the supreme Message-Light for humanity's perfection-life. Let us listen. We can listen. We must listen!

Hurtful is the outer adventure-
 capture-march.
Fruitful is the inner adventure-rapture-dive.

The outer world belongs to the supremacy-fighters. The inner world belongs to the oneness-lovers. God's ultimate Perfection-World will bless and embrace the oneness-lovers with fondness and pride, and reject and forget the supremacy-fighters.

God the creation, in breathless sound, asks God the Creator: "O where are You?"

God the Creator, in fathomless silence, replies: "I am inside your Oneness-Fulness-Peace-blossoming Dream-Reality."

1992

My sweet Lord Beloved Supreme, You are Your Immortality's Compassion-Height.

You are telling the sincerity-purity-gratitude-flooded inner world that its teeming follies will devotedly surrender to a volley of surprises, illumining and fulfilling, in the New Year, 1992.

My sweet Lord Beloved Supreme, You are Your Divinity's Justice-Light.

You are telling the insincerity-impurity-ingratitude-flooded outer world that its unsearching mind, unaspiring heart and unsurrendering life will be forced to drown in the ocean of endless sorrows.

My Lord, You are telling the aspiration-heart and the dedication-life of the world that they must accept You, please You and fulfil You in Your own Way and never, never in their own ignorance-volcano-way if they dare to dream of reaching the Golden Shore, the Transcendental

Vision of Your own Heart-Breath.

My Lord, my Lord, may I be permitted to beg You to grant me a blessingful boon in the New Year? Do give me the capacity to please You in Your own Way sleeplessly and breathlessly.

"My child, My Dream-Flower-child and my Reality-Fragrance-child, your willingness-heart is your capacity. Your willingness-heart is My Smile, My only Smile."

My sweet Lord Beloved Supreme, today You are our Golden Boat. Tomorrow You will be our Golden Shore.

1993

God is dreaming,
Newness singing,
Oneness blossoming,
Fulness dancing.

Hope no more gropes.
Life without slopes.
Splendid depths and heights
Transform bondage-nights.

1994

The Year of Supreme Choice:

> The aspiring heart's confident forward march
> or
> The doubting mind's imminent backward run.

> Swim in the ocean of oneness-delight
> or
> Sink in the sea of separation-night.

From the higher worlds, the divine beings want to illumine, protect and perfect the earth planet.

From the lower worlds, the ignorance-titans want to dominate the earth planet. Let us make our wise choice here and now.

In us is Divinity's peace-lover. In us is humanity's war-monger. The one we do not want to feed and cherish we must bring to the fore immediately and cast aside ruthlessly.

Because of our conscious and continuous blunders, we have compelled our poor Lord God to sleeplessly cry.

Stop we must! From this very moment we must please God in His own Way, for there can be no other way if happiness is our choice, peace is our choice, Infinity-Immortality's fulfilment is our choice.

1995

My Lord, my Lord, my Lord!
"My child, My child, My child!"

My Lord, my Supreme Lord, my only Lord!

This year my heart's streaming gratitude-tears have given me the unimaginable capacity to place at Your Forgiveness-Feet the sweet bloom of my love, the pure blossom of my devotion and the true fragrance of my surrender.
  "My child, My Infinity's Dream-child, My Immortality's Reality-child, this year I shall grow in you with My unfailing Newness-Hope-Sky and I shall shine through you with My rising Fulness-Promise-Sun."
  My Lord, I am perfect only when I have Your Happiness-Heart as my sleepless Companion.
  "My child, I am complete only when I have your oneness-life as My breathless companion."

My Lord, my only Lord, this year to You, only to You, I shall offer My Victory's crown.

"My child, you, only you, are My Victory's Throne."

1996

This is the year of the soul's dream-bloom-surprises and the heart's reality-blossom-astonishments.

The helplessness of the mind is nowhere.
The hopelessness of the heart is nowhere.
The uselessness of the life is nowhere.

The readiness of the inspiration-world-mind says to God: "Lord, I shall come."
The willingness of the aspirtion-world-heart says to God: "Lord, I am coming."

The eagerness of the dedication-world-life says to God: "Lord, I am come."

God blessingfully and proudly asks the *real* God-dreamer-mind to sing, the *real* God-lover-heart to dance, and the *real* God-server-life to smile and fly, fly and smile.

1997

The slow and long years of humanity's hope-heart shall begin to transform into humanity's fulfilment-life.

The beauty of world-peace was a sweet dream. The fragrance of world-peace shall begin to become a fruitful reality.

At long last the body shall offer its readiness, the vital shall offer its willingness, the mind shall offer its eagerness and the heart shall offer its oneness to the soul's God-Light-Manifestation and God-Delight-Satisfaction-tasks here on earth.

Earth's heart is smiling.
Heaven's Heart is singing.
Earth's breath is singing.
Heaven's breath is dancing.

I am saying to my Absolute Lord Beloved Supreme: "Father, my Father, I now have You."

My Absolute Lord Beloved Supreme is saying to me: "child, My child, you now I am."

1998

Peace, PEACE, Peace

My Peace is not the end of world wars.
My Peace is not the end of world-suffering.
My Peace is not the end of world ignorance.

Peace, PEACE, Peace

My Peace is the blooming beauty of my heart.
My Peace is the blossoming fragrance of my
   soul.
My Peace is my sleepless and breathless
ONENESS
With the Will
Of my Absolute Lord Beloved Supreme.

1999

My Lord Beloved Absolute Supreme
The sweet beginning of a new-dream-life –
The pure blooming of a new-hope-heart –
The sure blossoming of a new-promise-soul –

Humanity's self-discovery-boat shall ply
Between
Earth's newness-cry-shore
   And
Heaven's Fulness-Smile-Shore.

2000

The Absolute Lord Supreme
Tells the confusion-mind of the world:
"Take My Sadness-Heart and Madness-Eye
As the last and urgent Warning.
Come back Home immediately!"

The Beloved Lord Supreme
Tells the aspiration-heart of the world:
"In you is
My World-Transformation-Hope-Dream,
With you is
My Self-Transcendence-Vision-
  Manifestation-Promise
And for you is
My Smile-Beauty-Fragrance-Presence."

The Year Two Thousand
Is a decision-examination for humanity:
Either
We bind and blind the old world, and retire

Or
We embrace the new world of the forward
   march.
The Smile of the Beyond
Is beckoning us
To come and play hide-and-seek.

2001

Uncertainty-supremacy assails the world.
God's secret and sacred Will
In the world of the unknowable prevails.

The New Millennium is humanity's
   unhorizoned
God-surrender-victory
And
Divinity's most glorious earth-blossom-
   discovery.

2002

O Pilot of the New Year-Boat,
Do give my heart a new hope,
My life a new promise
And me a new assurance
That You are going to take me
To Your Golden Shore.

2003

My Lord Beloved Supreme,
May each and every human being
Of the world
Please You, only You,
In your own Way
In the Year 2003.

2004

My prayerful message:

At the end of a very long and uncertain Ignorance-flooded Night-Road, the Beauty of a New Hope and the Ecstasy of a New Promise shall unmistakably blossom.

2005

The New Year
Is the year of the
Mind-Astonishment,
Heart-Government
And
Life-Fulfilment.

2006

My Absolute Lord Beloved Supreme,
Please tell me what is going to happen
In this New Year.
"My child, keep quiet.
With My Transcendental Vision,
I shall give humanity
A new hope,
A new promise
And
A new receptivity-acceptance of life.
All the aspiring human beings here on earth
Must join Me.
I shall succeed.
I am bound to succeed."

2007

A blue-gold hope-bird is flying
In the heart-sky of humanity.

The Golden Shore is beckoning
The blooming God-life-seekers
And
The blossoming God-heart-lovers.

Before long, the world-mind-uncertainty
Will be buried in oblivion.

Before long, the world-heart-certainty
Shall start reigning supreme.

The mind's power-drum is surrendering
To the sweetness-flute of the heart.

The oneness-peace-realities shall devour
The world-division-hunger-dreams.

APPENDIX

BIBLIOGRAPHY

SRI CHINMOY:

– *New Year's Messages from Sri Chinmoy, 1966-1994*, New York, Agni Press, 1994.

– *New Year's Messages from Sri Chinmoy, 1995-2007*, New York, Agni Press, 2015.

Suggested citation key is: NYM

Table of Contents

1966	9
1967	11
1968	12
1969	16
1970	17
1971	18
1972	21
1973	23
1974	25
1975	26
1976	27
1977	28
1978	29
1979	30
1980	31
1981	32
1982	33
1983	34
1984	35
1985	36
1986	37
1987	38
1988	39
1989	42
1990	43
1991	45
1992	47
1993	49

1994	50
1995	52
1996	54
1997	55
1998	57
1999	58
2000	59
2001	61
2002	62
2003	63
2004	64
2005	65
2006	66
2007	67

The heart-traveller

1. Aspiration-Flames — Aspiration and God's Hour
2. A Sri Chinmoy primer
3. Everest-Aspiration
4. New Year's Messages from Sri Chinmoy (1966-2007)
5. Flower-Flames

www.ingramcontent.com/pod-product-compliance
Lightning Source LLC
Chambersburg PA
CBHW030309100526
44590CB00012B/577